Shades of Becoming

Poems of Faith Transition

Edited by Nancy Ross and Kristen R. Shill

Cataloging-in-Publication Data
Names: Ross, Nancy, 1980- editor. | Shill, Kristen, 1986- editor.
Title: Shades of becoming : poems of transition / edited by Nancy Ross and Kristen Shill.
Description: [United States] : [Nancy Ross and Kristen Shill], [2019] |
Identifiers: ISBN 9781099157448 (pbk.)
Subjects: LCSH: Faith--Poetry. | Ex-church members--Poetry. | Ex-church members--Church of Jesus Christ of Latter-day Saints--Poetry.
Classification: LCC PS595.R4 S53 2019

contents

introduction

When I experienced the most painful part of my faith transition and started attending a new church, I initially found set prayers and poems in the service to be unnerving. That discomfort was part of my religious baggage. My former faith community discouraged scripted prayers except for rituals performed by male members. Many thought that liturgy prevented a speaker from communicating divine will in the moment. My unfamiliarity with the candles, prayers, and hymns of my new church often made me question what I was doing in this strange new space. Over time, I found that the opportunity to borrow someone else's words was a relief when I had none.

On further investigation, I found poems that described grief and others that described faith. I couldn't find any collections that spoke to the painful processes of losing, mourning, and rebuilding a different kind of spiritual life. My hope for this collection is that it resonates with others who are also in this unfamiliar space of losing belief, certainty, and faith community—all those who experience rapid shift in worldview and the accompanying fallout.

The poems are divided into three stages of this journey: the early recognition of loss ("in the shallows"), the more developed feelings of grief and anger ("the deep end"), and emerging emotional resolution ("finding ground.").

Kristen and I offer them to you as a reassuring mirror: an affirmation of this particular kind of bereavement, with its many shades of loss and unsought but hard-won gifts of insight.

Nancy Ross

in the shallows

Nancy Ross
First Steps

Remainder of a recent rainfall
Innocent and narrow
Shallow-looking
Smooth, still water
I peered into it
Seeing only myself
At an awkward angle
I tapped my toe at its edge
"Stay out of there"
My mother warned.

Content in my perception
I jumped in with both feet.

It swallowed me whole.

Nancy Ross
A blessing for those who begin

You awake to discover
The fragility of your treasures
Held as precious by generations
Of revered foremothers
Who have nurtured you with their stories
Broken in the night
The shards of dead words scattered on the floor.

I bless you to sit
In the wreckage of this moment
Mourn the loss of this inheritance
Bid farewell, when you are ready,
To the heirlooms
No longer in your possession.
Sort through the remaining clutter
Of ideas and beliefs you've been gathering
Saving only that which is enduring
The anchors of a new collection
A fresh existence
It is a grievous but blessed beginning.

Coral Rose Goplin
(babel)

realizing you no longer
have a common vocabulary
with people you love
yesterday you were striving
towards the same heavenly expanse
hearts yearning in unison
but without a language
to talk to each other
adjectives to describe
verbs to propel
the everyday prepositions
begin to decline
in, towards, with, together,
among, around,
versus, excluding, against, outside.

Heather Harris-Bergevin
Godless

What do you do, when you
decide to leave
God's people? I've been
faithful, working in service
this whole life, and trust me,
that's a massive sacrifice, giving
my body in service to my Lord,
Baalam. Working in the temples is not
for the weaker believers. The rites
and rules must be closely followed, even
when they seem a bit strange to
Outsiders, offlanders □—but here came
this man, this Israelite, this Hosea, a man
named Salvation, who loved
me and wanted my hand, not
only my body in the sacred fertility
secret ceremonies. He wants to become
Ishi, my partner, my husband, to leave these,
my masters behind, to pay my
bride price, already high, because
I'm already bride and bridled to
these fellow temple workers. A slave
to my God, Baal, whom this man,
Ishi, says I shall no longer
worship, with either my
body of my soul? What other
God shall I speak with, now, Ashtarte
being forbidden, Baal
no longer in fashion, and my body
unaccustomed to the touch of only
one man-god within
or without the temple walls. I think,
Gomer, we could have, together,
a life, a child, and no more
trips to visit the midwife to take

care of little problematic repercussions
from hard work in the temple
till my legs ache. We could name
it "Jezreel:" as God scatters
his people, not only me, and I
will be just like everybody else, no
longer sanctified and consecrated to
God, except through this
man, Hosea, whose new God,
unfamiliar, surely
can take care of us?

J. Marie Murphy
Absolution

Defined,
Absolution is
A cleansing
A purification
An exoneration
Of the wrong-doings
The wrong-feelings
The wrong-choosings
That have preceded

Can we, however
Ever
Be absolved
Cleansed
Purified
Exonerated
Of the blemishes we've left
On hearts
That have come up against ours

Any skilled surgeon
Will use their hands
And tools
In such a way
As to produce
The least amount of scarring
Leaving as little evidence
of the trauma that existed
As their tools will allow

But even the most practiced of hands
Cannot guarantee
That we will be left markless
Even after the healing

And sometimes
In time
Scar tissue fades
And what once was a gaping wound
Becomes nearly imperceptible
On the map of our skin

Is time then,
More than,
"I'm sorry"
Or
More than
A jury's verdict
The only being with the power
To grant us our absolution

Is time then
The baptism for our grief?
Or our penance
For the grief we've caused

Maybe time then
Is the only real forgiveness

For it is only with
The arrival and passing of days
The orbits of the moon and sun
The waxing and waning of tides
That the scars our souls carry
Can ever
Be made whole

Holly Welker
Self-Portrait as Burnt Offering

The prophet says:
I have earned a right to the voice of prophecy.
I have suffered and seen the future
and suffered by the seeing.

I am neither a prophet nor
all that good at making things up as I go.
I speak in sensible tones.
I observe the present moment.
I record the moment's events.

I review the record and say,
Well, I suppose that is what happened.

I've learned this about memory: the fact that
I can't trust it doesn't mean I should forswear it.
The same is true of weather forecasts and prayer.

Early on I discovered an elemental preference,
the story I shy from all water and earth,
the one that intrigues me air and fire.

Jehovah, angry god of an angry desert, watched
smoke ascend to heaven. In that desert
the firstborn child had to be offered
as a sacrifice, or a sacrifice made in its place.

The second child you got to keep.

Smoke is Jehovah's offering, water
his weapon. He killed first by flood.

Movement starts from the center.
Smoke ascends, water falls. In
my desert and the desert of my forebears

our offering to God is
water: sweat spilled digging
reservoirs and irrigation canals,
the water flowing in them.
My ancestors vowed to make the desert blossom.
Prosperity became an offering but not a sacrifice,
the unretainable thing God demands you keep.

The prophets of landscape say:
our dams will outlast the water they hold.

Prophecy and history flow from the present.
I learned history and doctrine; I was
seared by probability and logic but
never by prophecy and faith. My parents'
second child, I would not be kept.
I made myself the sacrifice to be offered for the first—
a resentful gift evaporating like water in the desert,
leaving behind defiling blackness and a stench like smoke
from the charred timbers of a fallen church,
from a witch writhing in the stake's flames,
from a heap of smoldering books.
The God I was offered to can do nothing
with me but cast me away
and hope there is no other god to find me precious,
who will hand me back to my family and say,
Here, I know how to sacrifice too.

Cat Roebuck

I tried to tell my mother
what the shepherd did to me;
she said:
be still,
he may be God.

Cat Roebuck

I heard the shepherdess cry out
from the small veiled house she never leaves.

I heard her plead: "forbid them not
to come to me, let me speak comfort to their suffering."

the shepherd served a silent sacrament to her:
mutton, chops, lamb tongues boiled and cut,
adorned with bitter herbs.

she fell quiet, and the flock did too.

Mark Jeffreys
Faith

I believe that the dead are
As "banal as the living."
I believe that they exist
In the same spaces we do,
Bounded by rounded squash skulls
In part, and by submerged streams
Descending through mists of art

Such as language and picture
And community dances,
In part. We commune with them
So unsatisfyingly
But so well, as we commune
With ourselves, and I have faith
As we are, we are lonely.

Holly Welker
Bad Habits

I have books I've never read,
and I buy more.
This makes me sad,
so I imagine I will read them all
in a burst of desperate determination
when I reach a place without bookstores.

It's not that there are no bookstores,
it's that the place is an island.
No, it's not that the place is an island,
it's that I make my house into an island
and pretend I can't leave.
That's when I start reading.

The story doesn't go any further than that.
OK it's not that the story doesn't go further,
it's that I'm afraid to admit
all that's left to me is hope
for a happy ending.
Hope confuses me always.

It's not that hope confuses me,
it's that it leads to other confusing things.
Hope in a right thing leads to dissatisfaction:
everyone else tries to convince you
your hope in a right thing
is really all wrong.

You can try to be strong if you like.
It doesn't matter:
one day when you're tired of sleeping,
bored by the weather and finished with your books,
your hope in a right thing will turn into
hope in a wrong thing.

It's not that hope in a right thing
turns into hope in a wrong thing,
it's that hope is a habit
as hard to break and useless
as remembering the phone number
of the house you lived in as a child,

it's not even that hope is a habit,
it's that hope is a garment
that fits you and fits you
until you awaken one morning
thinner and shorter
and suddenly dressed in despair.

Nancy Ross
Embodiment

Fear is in there
Joanna said
Deep in the spleens
Of white women
Sealed away in the good tupperware
Safe from encounter or influence

Under containers of
Rage
Courage
Pleasure
Sorrow
Floating in a soup of
Explanations and justifications
I found my fear

Reacquainted with the
Undiluted strength of
Flavorful feelings
I scraped off
The smiling veneer of orthodoxy
Feasting with tears and regret
On all I had denied myself
On all that was forbidden.

Jennith Lucas
Mormon Style Glory

A house of golden bricks, Cumorah unearthed
Collapsed in mineral distress, a pocketful
of pyrite. I testified upon the pew
my father whispered in my ear—red velvet
and lacy white hand-me down dress—"I know…"
who knew you never did know—believing in gods
disguised as friends, if you play the games they choose.
Ancient scriptures translated into your mother's dreams,
the size of planets, god-soaked,
Eternal transcendence in interstellar glory
damnation the color of menstrual blood
charting maritime paths from fibula to temple.
in hell, you do not burn, because you live
eternally separated from those you love.

this quarter made of fool's joy is flying
on heads, tails or unknown sides,
it never hits the surface of my palm.

Holly Welker
Christian Art

Saint Paul, who is often painted balding
        and glum, told us, "If there be
                any virtue, if there be any praise,
                        think on these things."
Christine who's an idiot and not really
        my friend called "L'Eglise de Jeanne d'Arc"
                the "Jeannie Dark Church"
        which is cool actually
                in its own particular way.
The theme is particular vices: strands
        of beads and heavy brass earrings, skulls,
                roses wilted in a vase, pomegranates
                        oozing red juice, a map of the world
                with America a yellow bar surrounded
                        by blue, your reflection
                                in a mirror because
Saint Paul also wanted all of us dressed
        in the armour of light which Jeanne d'Arc
                put on in the end and perhaps it protected
        her and perhaps it only hurt.
It has to be enough to make you feverish
        and ill but in a good way, really,
in a way that your cheeks are always flushed
        and nothing ever tastes good enough
                to eat so you forget how to
                        swallow and remember only
                to sing and that's how you generate
                        your own astonishment
                at the tangled way life funnels down
                        to a dark painful source
                                of envy and praise.
Well that's that! Somewhere some people
        are singing Gregorian chants a capella
                in monkish tenor voices and if I
                        could find anything to envy I'd envy

it with anxious deliberation,
I'd praise light so busy and abundant
its surplus breeds wonder and
pleasure and over-indulgence
and ends in a sudden flash of
blindness
that never goes away

Nancy Ross
My God

I am exhausted from the lifelong worship
Of a fragile idol of factory-made ceramic
That chips and cracks from lustful thoughts and swear words
Whispering into my ear judgements
On the weakness of my character
As I attempt a perfect obedience
In return for promises of eternal servitude
An unbalanced trade of the damned
With little hope for redemption.

Mark Jeffreys
Spookism

Culture is the abode of God,
The home of all souls. Words
Were the beginning of whole
Numbers, of whole worlds,
Of wholes. Nothing was part
Or parcel of other . . . Oh.
I don't know. The creek
At the top of the scenic road
Through Zion runs free.
All the dams well below.
Turkey and deer, also tourists
In rental cars and on bicycles,
Crowd its ever-crumbling shores.
Cross over, cross over,
Drink your fill. Mists and snow
Wraith the sheer canyon walls.
Rocks from fires, water
From the rock, life
From water, word
From the lives tumbling out, God,
Spirits and spooks of all kinds,
The thermodynamic cascade.
We were always correct, reading
Faith backward, immaterial
And material are linked after all,
Only it's the latter started higher,
Up in those seraphic veils.
You can't resist. You're a tear
On a tear down the cliffs,
A momentary swirl
In the words for the world
That return as your soul,
Braid of old words pooling,
Passing through the momentary
Vortices of you, downhill.

Cat Roebuck

after his fast,
the Good Shepherd broke
a lamb;
"this is *my* flesh," he said, tearing its limbs,
"this is *my* blood," he said as it spilled.
He ate, and called it
good.

the deep end

Holly Welker
Sentence

You lie like a comma in the sentence of your bed.
Your legs stack like planks;
each hand steadies the opposite shoulder.
It's a position you assume when
assailed by dreams or sleepless longing,
or on nights you feel you're breathing
broken glass. Tonight you buckle into
yourself and mourn two vocabularies,
a moldy discourse you outgrew
and a fluent address you never learned.
The prayers of your childhood
quite frankly suck, you conclude,
rote requests that sugary red punch
and chocolate donuts somehow
strengthen and nourish bodies always
prone to sin, and perfunctory pleas
that no harm or danger might fall over
you, as if you were a gnarled root
obstructing a path. At least you
learned to plunder an ordinary day
for blessings worth acknowledging,
so you release a long breath and start a list:
Lord, I thank you for spring,
for the crisp steady light of May and
the many varieties of lilacs.
Also for my opposable thumbs,
which so often come in handy,
and that really nice port
I had last week at my cousin's.
Please bless me with a loving heart.
A loving heart? You hadn't known
you could pronounce such a sentence.
The words jangle in the dark
like a drawer of kitchen knives
rattled by a ghost. Who asks for

such a thing? You do, apparently.
You're horrified at your
sentimentality, your audacity,
and the fact that you took so long
to realize you'd like to junk
the ire and indignation you've
draped for decades across your
shoulders like a vainglorious yoke
you sentenced yourself to carry.
What would grace feel like, finally?
Like the air around a wondrous
sentence spoken into the dark as you
wait for another sentence to follow?

J. Marie Murphy
Absolution II

Someone asked me once
On a day cooled with self-shaming
If I was looking for absolution
"Do you seek absolution"
Their words, verbatim

And in reply?
My words?
Verbatim,
No.
No, I do not wish for absolution

Absolution
Is like bleach
Chemically
whitewashing everything it touches
Restoring a white, bright T-Shirt
or
Destroying a beloved pair of blue jeans

And I have never been
Nor do I aspire to be
A white, bright T-Shirt

I have always been
Indigo dyed
Woven threads
Of denim

And I think I prefer it that way it that way

You see,
It is much too hard to be a white T-Shirt

Life as a white t-shirt means:
Foregoing chocolate ice cream cones
Or wooded, muddy hikes
Remaining in the closet during summer barbecues
Or spaghetti dinners warm with companionship
Knowing full well
That any white shirt will need replacing at the tiniest of stains

But denim?
Oh yes, let me be denim every day

Denim can ramble on hilltops,
Wrestle in the barn
Sit on the ground during a lazy afternoon picnic
Bask in sunbaked naps on summer grass
And even a most favored pair of jeans
Can get worn
And faded
And hem-torn

And they are
To their wearer
Still worthy

The blemishes even
Giving them character
Telling of the stories and adventures
That you,
That those jeans,
have been a part of

So yes,
let me be denim
And no,
It isn't absolution I seek

What I seek
Is acceptance
The acceptance of my flaws

And misdeeds
And missteps
And stains, covering my whiteshirtedness
Like a blood-seeping wound

Let me be denim
And
Let me be worthy
Let me be worthy and forgiven
Let me be worthy and forgiven in my faded, fraying state
Let me be worthy
Without
Bleach

Heather Harris-Bergevin
To whom will you go:

God will always find you, or rather
will if you are searching. God doesn't
care what name or race you call
her, or whether you believe he
is a being or a universe or nebulous
wizard bard to your
protagonal wishes. He just
Is, and if you want to find
Them, to locate what
She wants you to do in your life, it might
be a good option to no longer care
what the face of God looks like,
binary or non
black or white or tan, but see the Face
in those around you.   Some of the most
Christian people I know, who serve
the face of God in the poor, the face
of God in the homeless, the face of
God in the abused, are, after all,
atheistic, not waiting around for
thoughts and prayers magical thinking,
but, seeing what needs doing, shouldering
the sounds and souls of others, and getting
to work.   I want to work as hard
as a good atheist, pray as hard as a
sinner saved, as we are all sinners,
and saved by the hand of God, unrelenting,
despite the things we attempt in Their names,
despite our discourse over whether she lives or
He saves, despite our doubt and despite our
dreams, still the love goes, flows, and we
open our sieve hands wide, guzzling,
wondering if we can scrabblegrasp enough,
when she, pouring wisdom, shakes their
head, and smiles, and teaches his babies how

to properly hold the cup.

Susan Meredith Hinckley
Misunderstanding

Does a bird wonder
if it is enough? It does what it
was made to do, it lives
its life of bird-thanks
on the wind, eyes black
and tuned to tiny things despite
an endless sky, each second
just a beat to stay alive,
its thoughts of stick
and seed, it sings for daylight
not to beg forgiveness
for its bird-ness, fancy dances
for a mate and lays a cache of secrets,
teaches all the work of wings but
carries just itself.

And God lets birds be birds,
pleased at His creation.

It is good.

But I must wonder
how I've learned
to count my own lack, wonder
how I missed the point of birds, that
clearly, Being is enough.

Josie Chilton
The Questions

Who will attend to my gaping wounds
When no-one believes they exist?

How can I feel the strength of my hand
When they've cuffed me at the wrist?

Why do I hope they will change their hearts
When again and again I get burned?

When will I stop craving their love
When it's the kind that has to be earned?

What do I do when they tell me I'm bad
And yet demand that I stay?

Where do I go to find what I had
Before it all went away?

Mette Ivie Harrison
Stone For Bread

I prayed for answers.
Why did this happen to me?
Why did my daughter die?
Why didn't I get the miracle?

Silence from God.

A friend told me that I had to keep asking.
She told me I needed to pray louder.
Longer, harder, deeper,
To read my scriptures more,
And to fast more.
She told me God does not give a stone,
When you ask for bread.

I wanted bread.
Glutenous, delicious, hot, steaming
Bread fresh from the oven.
Dripping in butter,
The best thing in the world.

I wanted bread,
Not a stone.
But I got a stone.
And somehow,
I am still trying to figure out
What kind of God gives
A stone.

Cat Roebuck

when the harvest is good,
the master feasts on his disciples,
sheep who trust his voice,
fish who trust his silence,
bread baked from plump wheat.

when the sun withdraws,
the master wraps in wool to rest
pillowed on straw.

Holly Welker
Dynamics

The manuscript illuminating the fall of the rebel angels
reveals that things must cease to be what they are
for the angels are no longer graceful or clean;
they lack wings to lift themselves from hell
which yawns below them: the mouth of a mongrel dog.

The rebel angels asked, "Why should God be always
God? Even Music Television has at least the *appearance*
of change," and so were damned. If the imagination
is anything it is a prism, and hell is life
without it: a place where things turn into
what they already are: chairs become chairs, music
is always Mozart.

In the miracle of birth what should be one becomes two.
In the tragedy of stasis what should be one becomes
nothing worth saving. If the imagination is a prism,
pain coats it with sticky grime, any light refracted
as gray and unwavering as suffering in hell,

where travel is always at night and by train,
the windows too grimy to reveal to the demons, angels
and bored listless humans whose heads rest against them
the damp rocky landscape. So passengers ransack
their minds for curses they have never been taught.
Passengers have as well no word for *dissatisfaction*
or even *lack*; their own names remain for them
as ineffable as even God declared his name,
the language of need a dark angry stain on the flat sky
pressing itself wetly to the train.

Susan Meredith Hinckley
Geology Lesson

My faith is a stone so heavy
I cannot move it, angels must
roll it away. Sometimes
the tomb is empty
sometimes it guards its secret, alive
or dead—I cannot know. I stroll
a liminal garden, I wait,
shame and sorrow wrapped
in the same linen I use to keep
wonder and hope.

My faith is a stone skipping lightly across seas,
if thrown just right.

Mossy faith, slick in the bottom of a ditch,
irrigation rushing over it, spreading life
to my rows of everything, and all
my planted seeds. The weeds
grow too. My faith dries out,
waits for its next turn.

Sometimes I fish it from my shoe,
begin to walk but find it underfoot again.

Faith clumsy as a rock, sized
for my pocket, pebble faith passed
one hand to another, mine
to mine to mine. Today I am set down,
tomorrow I'm picked up again.

This is all I've learned.

Brittany Sweeney-Lawson
CTR

Choose the right, they say
Well, what if that means choosing
to leave all I've ever known?

Coral Rose Goplin

leaving
bearing on our shoulders
the remainders
all that has not been consumed
behind it smolders
dampened but perhaps not
entirely snuffed
and we carry
hope
that kindling
speaking of other fires
other hearths
other welcomes
despite the wreckage
ruin in our wakes.

Mette Ivie Harrison
When I Prayed Again

I wanted to believe in God again.
But when I knelt down, I felt nothing.
No kind father waiting,
No savior who had marks on his hands,
No magician who would wave a wand
And give me all the things on my list.

So I prayed the only thing I could think to pray.
I prayed, "I don't believe you are there."
I got no answer. Silence.
Though they say God answers every prayer,
I prayed again. I prayed each night
This same prayer for nearly a year.

And then at last I got an answer, one
I could hear.
"I am here," was all it said.
A warm feeling.
No window shaking.
No bush burning.
No cloud overhead.
No storm on the sea.

Heather Harris-Bergevin

The pope decided
God's love was big enough
that even divorced people
could receive the Holy
Sacraments, and all
Hell broke loose. People
protesting. Filing documents
charging him with heresy. Because
the Atonement is a miraculous divine sacrament
capable of wiping away all of
your pain, your sin, your
disappointment, your
infidelity, but not
a divorcee's.

Cat Roebuck

farmers save seeds, not souls—
the sickled field sorted,
chaff tossed to the pigs,
wheat hidden through winter,
buried to raise a new crop.

Brittany Sweeney-Lawson
Fistfight with God

I believe it's your turn to throw the next punch,
I think the bruises 'round my eyes have healed
And I know there's still a couple teeth left
up there in my mouth somewhere
It's your turn; I already gave it a try
But I missed you by, like, a mile
Bishop Thomas says I swung too wide,
came back and slugged my own insides
A cavity where a heart once was and only half a liver now
The rest was eaten up by cancer or
one of those plagues You like so much
As a matter of fact, I burped the other day and a frog crawled
out of my mouth, hopped onto my plate and ate
the rest of my tuna fish sandwich
That sounds about right
So come on, no gloves off, round two, round three
Let's make you feel my misery
I'm punching at You with all I'm worth,
but all I get for all my trouble is hunger and exhaustion
and a really bad case of shoulder cramps
Just socking, screaming, swearing that way really takes it out of
          me
So I'm going to bed now, You hear?
But only for a little while,
some of us need our sleep
But don't You worry, I'll be back tomorrow
And while I lay me down, if you could just do me a solid,
to give me a fair shake next time □ —
Keep out the burglars, bad dreams, sickness
Make sure I don't fall out of bed and break my arm or something,
Then I'll be ready; I'll be in top form
So I'm giving You fair warning:
Watch Your back,
Cuz when I come back,
I won't go easy; I'll come out swingin'

Coral Rose Goplin

last night i dreamt you welcomed me
back into your home and church
i was scared that you could see
my heart
torn to shreds by God's love
by a masculine force as determined
to control my
body
vagina
mind
vagina
soul
as His hands and feet on earth.

i am brutalized
i stand before you knowing
you preferred me silent.
malleable.
victimized.

Holly Welker
Conversation of the Universe

Prime, prim and primitive,
you want to be them all,
like Eleanor Roosevelt's
uncanceled face on a twenty-cent stamp,
ready, ready to go.
Once a pencil box told you to
Create the Future with Your Eyes and Legs,
now the *Nude Reclining* in March reminds you that
your lover dreams of your hips and aches
to drink wine from your mouth,
but here is April's water color:
daffodils and boiled eggs
and a lovely silver creamer,
and you think it needs a plus sign
because shouldn't even a still life
add up to something?

Someone puts rum in your tea.
Ask for two flavors of frozen yogurt,
the counter person offers it to you either
twisted or side by side
as if it were love.
The stuff we skim off the surface of life:
lyrical and capable of great enchantment
like a salamander slick with its own fire.
Seduce is a marvelous word
but something got crushed for two and a half decades
and now you watch the gradual emancipation
of a treasure inside yourself,
not sex and not pleasure,
but pretending and pleasure in the pretense.

What happened to the night you lifted triumphantly over your
        shoulders,
intending to toss it in the Dumpster,

to brush dust from your hands as you walked away?
Now the echo of your shout for help falls
in syncopated clicks of consonants
that bounce off walls and settle in mounds.
You're following directions but you look silly
surrounded by porcelain letters
and alphabet building blocks,
you're afraid of dying far from home
and settling into the uneven sediment of history
before anybody even knows of your forays
into the land of wax and wicks and shadow.

Can a terraced island offer any protection
besides the broad curved canopy of the sky?
Gazing through your brother's telescope,
you didn't see anything that wasn't blurry and too large,
anything that made you any less certain
that being alone is the very best thing to wish for.
The moon is the only thing you can trust in the sky:
it's too busy finding new ways to look at itself
to bother checking up on us.
Full, it hangs in the night
like a great big period:

conversation of the universe
                    stops here.

C.M.Blanco
'I AM NOT'

As Eve was deprived.
Of herself in the flow
By God.
Still I am

A metanarrative I do not longer
belong to.
Yet, ay!, how much I've loved Thee.
Backwards. Fly.
Taking a body. Raped us of our stories.
Chain it down.

I am not a woman
Nor do I wish to a man be.
I'm being written.
Still I am.

Higgledy, piggledy, my black hen
He lays eggs for gentlemen.
Did you hear?
I am.

Up the river, Up the river, Up the river
Did not ask.
just wanna go back to New York.
Downtown.

My left veins always seemed so plausible:
Still untouched.

Do not abort me
by the size of my womb.
As my back archens
I am.

Such a silence such a sound.
Sleep us so… hush, hush, hush.

A work in progress.
Unfinished.

I'll celebrate
Frac-ture

It never was so
(   )
Walking through
a flowered
dead Elah.

Through my braided hair time sleeps.
Transitory mental derangement,
Still I am.

I am not my
(own) body.
I am not truly one but truly multitudes.
And even
if in the despairing realms of Bedlam I am to be awaited
I am (not).
I am (not).
I am.

Mette Ivie Harrison
Mother's Blessing

She puts her hands on my head
By the power of the divine womanhood we both share,
And blesses me to love myself, to love others,
To feel power in moving forward,
To see clearly, and kindly.

She blesses me to see Her
Within myself, and within others,
To see Her face when I look in the mirror,
And when I am angry and afraid
Around my sisters and brothers.

She blesses me to let go of past hurts,
And past fears, to dance and sing freely,
To create art that is true and good,
To be the mother I never had,
And always wished for.

Then when she is done with the blessing,
She passes me the oil and tells me it is my turn.
She kneels in front of me,
And waits as I am astonished that she believes
I can do this for her.

Coral Rose Goplin
Alchemy

they've spent yearsdecadeslifetimes
attempting to change
one into the other
we scoff at early chemists
ignorance of truths
proven by geniuses we will never be
they thought rumpelstiltskin
was
a chemical reaction they could
master
straw to gold a fairytale
base metal into gold, though
transmutation turned myth…
fools.
we do not mince words
these men who once believed
in an earth-centric universe
a world with edges

and yet
i've seen us spend yearsdecadeslifetimes
attempting to change
inequality into equality
transmutation
via gospel.

Jeannine Robinett
Reclamation

I thread the needle yet again,
And tie the knot that will keep
The thin white thread
Firmly in the fabric.

Examining the gaping hole,
I wonder, is it really worth
The effort of repair?

It is not mending,
But reweaving,
Finding new ways of linking
These frayed, distant edges.

Once is not enough.
I double or triple knot,
Hoping it will be enough.

Laura Leigh
The Spirit
(2015)

I arrived with broken heart;
a front-row contrite spirit if ever there was one.
I ate the flesh of Jesus Christ,
drank his blood right on down,
and waited patiently for the spirit to be with me—
for that bosom-borne burning I'd been promised.
(*Bosom*, LOL)
Anywayyyy,
the cannibalization of our Lord and Savior
did not result in the spirit befalling me
at that particular moment

Brother Jeppsen testified
about how he'd been struggling, so
he opened his Book of Mormon
TO THE EXACT SCRIPTURE HE NEEDED
AT THAT EXACT MOMENT
and felt the spirit.
I thought I'd give it a go—
closed my eyes and turned to the very special verse Jesus wanted
me to see.
(OMG there is an app for that)

"Their dead bodies were heaped upon the face of the earth
...So great was the scent thereof"

Jesus, that's dark.
My bosom burneth notteth,
But my stomach rumbled mightily
(from all that fasting)
(not to disfigure my face or whatever).
Maybe there was something lost in translation
and the Lord God really meant
aboral peristalsis

and Smith et al. just misunderstood.
(It could happen to anyone).

I walked home
with broken heart.
Brokener than before.

Later,
I sat in a botanical garden on a blanket:
base of a mountain,
wildflowers all around,
stars lighting the stage.
The band appeared
The music started
The singer sang a simple hymn

A barony of ivy in the trees
Expanding out its empire by degree

A lump caught in my throat
A series of neuronal electrical signals
A synaptical heyday.
I felt God everywhere
I felt alive in the spirit
My cup runneth over

And so,
my brothers and sisters,
I'd like to bear my testimony of Colin Meloy.

J. Marie Murphy
Donna

It's easy to break hearts, you know,
Leaving religion behind
And no one really wants to know, you know,
How you're doing when they bump into you
Next to the frozen peas
"We really should get together sometime!"
Not a lie
Exactly

And no one is really a liar
And no one feels like sinner
Until they're sitting across the couch from grandma
And she asks
"You still go to church,
Don't you?"
That comma, holding the weight of the only right answer
Her eyes, earnest with eternal, maternal concern

"Of course, grandma"
A lie
Exacting

Her eyes relax as she sits,
Tidily comforted
Reassured
As she fussed over her small chicks

Who am I to break her heart, honestly?
A more genuine answer, selfish with honesty

No, grandma
I haven't been to church in years
And I don't intend to, ever, honestly
A truth

What penance is appropriate for a lie to your grandmother?
Confession?
Repentance?
How many *Hail Marys*
Make up for sinning against a kind woman,
bathed in 60 watt light,
60 years of marriage,
60 grandchildren?

If I were to confess, it'd be to this

I confess that her heart may not have broken
But mine did

Broke knowing
How she must've been systematically
Disrespected
And overlooked

Broke knowing
Her clever mind and sharp sensibilities
Were ignored
Her skills patronized

My heart breaks for the tidy woman,
Comfortable shrouded in floral wallpaper
Comfortable shrouded in the fog of patriarchal righteousness

Her heart may not have broken,
But mine did

I don't even have to know her story
To know her story

Don't we all
All of us women
Birthed or bred into piety
Saddled with scripture
Have a version of the same story?

The demented fanfiction of some sky-deity or other

A mercy?
Or a sin?
To not offer another heartbreak
On the altar
Of the coming and going
Between
The Faithful and *The Unbelieving*

I'd pray
If I prayed
That her god
Would think it a mercy

A truth

Coral Rose Goplin

if i tell you
the bone-deep lonely
of losing my faith
you feel vindication
and offer a sermon
on the body of Christ
and communion of the saints
you remind me i
pruned myself off the
Tree of Life
which awaits my regraft.

but the saints never
communed for me
as they seem to do for you.
they observed me with their Christ
forming judgments as dull blades
chopping bluntly slowly methodically

i was never sure how
this bounty of
Rules
spring from
Grace
how these fruits produced
proclaimed Great Hope

be Feminine.
be Modest.
be Pure and Chaste and Sweet.

bone-deep in Adam's Rib
their cuts reverberated
and as i fell
alone
severed free
i realized

there was never a place
in that Orchard
for Me.

Mette Ivie Harrison
See You In Hell

I used to sit in church and think every time
someone said something I didn't believe in,
Well, I guess I'm going to hell for that, too.
There were a lot of things that I was going to hell for.
Same-sex marriage destroying the family,
And women needing to stay in their place,
And needing to never criticize the leaders.

I'd imagine myself falling into hell and burning there,
Even though I know that Mormons don't believe in hell.
I'm pretty sure they think that people like me
Will go there anyway, because God will create one
Just to show me how wrong I am.

And then I started to realize there were lots of other people
Who seemed to be happily going to hell.
They were people I liked and wanted to spend time with.
They said they'd be right there with me,
If we all went to hell,
And we'd all have a grand old time.
Maybe our hell is better than some people's heaven.

Maren Chen
Storage

How much space do you have in your apartment? Your dorm
room? Your house? Your basement?

How much space do you have in your heart? Your mind? Your
soul? Your conscience?

Do you have room for the wheat that will never be eaten? For the
questions that will never be answered?

Will you keep it all, year after year, nicely labeled and organized?
Contents and date.

Wheat. Potato Pearls. Rice. Powdered Milk. (The label says
"1994," but you're sure it's still good.)

Polygamy. The Temple. The Priesthood Ban. The Policy. (You
know which one, but if a date is needed, you will write
"November, 2015" on the label.)

Perhaps these cans, these questions,
Will be passed on to future generations
Who will have to decide
What to do with them.

What to do with this can of wheat? Keep it? Eat it? (Surely not.)
Throw it out? (But that is wasteful.) Give it to someone who will
appreciate it?

What to do with this question, this doubt? Keep it? Hold on to it?
Or let it go? Throw it in the trash? (But oh, what would your
pioneer ancestors say to such waste?)
Give it to someone who still has room on her shelf? Someone who
still has a shelf?

Uneaten food. Unanswered questions.
(Inedible food. Unanswerable questions.)

What will you do with this heritage?

Mark Jeffreys
What the Doll in the Fairytale Said

We doubt. Doubt is the best clue
Our evolved brains vouchsafed us.
Doubt is what makes us

Squint at the moon, paint in caves,
Pierce flutes, write poems, throw bones.
We vacillate between faith
What we do matters,

That it matters if we win,
If we impress each other,
If we assert our control,

And doubt, why we dream fictions.
"This world? I think there may be
Something wrong with it,
Something underneath."

Allison Ulrich

These walls
Covered in textures of my tradition, rough and woven
Place of parting with my mom's deceased body
        of memorializing her in story and song
Place in which I first donned pants for worship
        and openly fed my nursing child
Place in which I sat and watched as men circled my daughter to
        give her a name and a blessing
        in which I stood to capture that daughter two years later as
        she ran to catch up with her dad
        who stood to bless my son, encircled again by men
Walls in which I used my hesitant voice for the first time
        and held my head high in a place of worship for the first
        time
        taught adults the good news for the first time
Walls in which I spoke openly about faith and doubt, joy and pain,
        love, isolation, questions, and disappointments
Walls in which while in deep grief due to acts of exclusion by
        those in power
        I sobbed and begged my sisters and brothers to sit with
        those hurting
Walls in which my will to be the change from within waxed
        and waned
Walls in which I've felt simultaneously right at home
        and pushed out
Walls in which I thought my children would be submerged in
        water to show their love for God
        but in which I now hope they don't
These walls
        have betrayed me

65 the deep end

finding ground

Mette Ivie Harrison
Endless Pit

I wasn't pushed.
I didn't fall.
It feels like I stood at the precipice for a thousand years,
Weighing the pros and cons,
Imagining the fall,
Arguing and explaining
With my husband
And my children.

But when the time came,
I jumped alone
Into the endless pit.
I am still falling,
Waving my arms,
Screaming
And kicking my feet.

So why did I jump?
I chose because it had to be.
I don't claim a serpent tempted me.
This wasn't a fall.
It was a leap into the unknown.
This was the divine in me,
Wanting to experience the
Good and bad, the bitter and sweet,
The glory and terror.

Keira Shae
Sacred Wild

Someone told me to stand in holy places;
I think it's necessary to have wild spaces.
Where time is measured in centuries and eons.
Where you hear from your heart, not the throngs.

Wild's where you can make your choices carefully
Among the calling, the mating, and bearded barley,
You will feel so small and nature humbles you right;
Marvel at your place under the stars this night.

Kristen R. Shill
The Loneliness of God

On the first day,
She baked bread
pounded together of starflour—
hope as leavening,
yeasty anticipation of new heights
to counterpoise Her depths.

On the second, She took a walk.
The weather was fine,
and She was tired,
tickled Her feet on eddies
of darkness and lightness,
and it was well.

The morning of the third,
She slept in,
sipped Her coffee thoughtfully,
looked out at the worlds She grew
and wondered if they were bored, too.

The fourth came and went in the garden.
She named the favorite plant Daphne,
watering her with the Word.
She seduced the lilies with song,
wove arias to the rhubarb,
kitchen witch to comfrey and calendula.

The fifth, She put up Her feet.
Omniscience is thirsty work,
and the vein of her Vine
ran thick and heady.
She drank her own good health.

On the sixth, She was lonely.
Part sculptor part scientist,

She knitted them of sorrows and strings,
planted them with longing they could not name
in Her garden.
She said
Be kind! Be happy.
Inhabit this place I have made.
I deny you nothing.
You will see Me in each other's faces
(I made you in my image),
and when your faces become mirrors
of my grace to one another,
you must leave me.
You will no longer need me.

On the seventh day, She wept
and began again.

Alisa Bolander
November 9, 2016

I can't resist the gentle glimpse of heat
Easing itself through the eastern glass door

I walk out, sole skin on sandpaper concrete
The birds, high and unseen

They're talking to each other
Singing about the morning, as if it were something new

I wasn't expecting the grass to be warm in November
Although it's lumpy, and I slowly crush a brown leaf

Crusty, crumbling beneath the ball of my foot
It grew waxy and green all summer, before

Any of this was known
Although nothing here seems to know it

I expertly slide a dandelion stem through my toes
A tuft bunches and disintegrates on top

I let the fliers go upwind of my lawn
There's bound to be the same struggle next year anyway

My shadow is twice my height
It's not ten in the morning

I stand, my arms akimbo, feeling the curves of a woman's body
My legs planted wide and strong

Far west
A passenger jet flies south over Herriman

I turn my face a quarter
And become Janus, half alight with the future

Half darkened by the past
The poet said it is a serious thing

To be alive on this fresh morning
In this broken world

Across the street a neighbor whistles twice, quickly
For his young dog to come out

I go around back through the north gate
Onto ice-water grass

To call for my outdoor friends

Susan Meredith Hinckley
Babel

God speaks to us in any language
we can understand
God in birds, in trees
in wind, tall grass, its whisper
and its bend
words smooth as rain, or the embrace

of silence, eyes
or faces, seeds so small
they reach the places words can't go
at all

God in pie, if it's the kind my grandma made
God in the dishwater slipping through her hands
after we were filled, God in the suds
and in the song she hummed

Listen.

Coral Rose Goplin
losing faith

like i misplaced it and it now resides
in that dusty junk drawer of my heart under
old birthday candles and unpaired gloves
and twist ties in various colors.

no, i birthed this faithlessness
long contractions growing in intensity
pain. anguish. despair.
the tearing away of something nurtured and
sustained so long
until it is

separate

no longer mine.

Stephanie Sorensen
Bricks

My childhood home,
Seemingly unshakeable,
has come undone
Slowly—bit by bit.

What started as a broken pane
A crack in the wall
has turned into a pile of rubble
Bricks
Endless bricks

I pick one up and see
A familiar word etched deeply
in the stone
"Priesthood" it reads,
Heavy to hold.
"The Holy Ghost" catches my eye
Much lighter, maybe even weightless.

Then "Joseph Smith" comes into view
I hold that one a long, long time...
And juggle the rough-edged "Prophets"
And "Personal Revelation," too.

One by one, into the sorting piles
These bricks get placed:
RECYCLING or
RUBBISH
Until it's all been cleared

But for one lone brick
"Love"
It's clutched tightly to my chest
I set off eager to rebuild—
New walls. New floor.

New paint. New decor.
But never again a ceiling.

Only my house collapsed, after all.
Not me.

Sarah Broat
Of Hearts and Boxes

I saw you and my soul lit up
God said *no*
The Church said *no*
But my heart said *yes*

Hearts are notorious liars
Weaving dangerous fantasies that
Burn hot and fierce in the
Dim light of the lone and dreary world

So my heart, bright and shy
Went into a box
Onto a shelf bearing your name
And I settled for *good enough*

Daily it beat, pulsing
With fine golden rays of hope
For a future I could never have
If increase was my goal

I forged a sturdy lock
From my cruelest thoughts
You are a beloved child of God
And this is the path you chose

I swaddled my heart in every wish
And dream I had when we spoke
As I buttressed the shelf with
A bitter resin of my own design

They say families can be together forever
Can—not will
And if your shelf, my shelf broke
What starlight would I forfeit?

Yet my heart was not the liar
It was a solitary point of honesty
Waiting patiently for me,
Safe and protected in its box

What I found within
When I was brave enough
To open it was
A scorching flame

That burned down my shelf
And led me
Like a beacon
Back to you.

Mette Ivie Harrison
Nothing Is Forever

They say that families are forever.
But you wake up one day and realize that nothing is forever.
The Seven Wonders of the World aren't.
They're all going to collapse someday.
Not this year or next, but soon, probably because of global
        warming.
Even the sun isn't forever. It will expand and encompass the whole
        earth.
We'll all be gone by then, of course.
And eventually, the universe will be gone, too.
There will probably be another Big Bang,
But who knows what will come after that?
Not us.

Nothing is forever.
There are only moments,
Brief glimpses into happiness.
Of course, the whole idea of consciousness is a lie.
And so is the idea of your personality.
You are made up of impulses and memories that aren't real
And you aren't you.
That's a fiction as much as forever is.
But hold onto it for a little while.
Be who you are.
Hold your family close.
Nothing is forever.
Maybe nothing is real.
And still.

J. Marie Murphy
Absolution III

Can you
Can any of us
Be the giver of absolution
For a grievance that isn't yours to bear?
For scars and pain
That you did not inflict?

We don't often get the chance
To wrestle with our surgeons, do we?
We are sent home
Post-op, post incision, post scarring
And those around us Get to deal with the scars

Or
We deal with them on our own
As well as we can
Until someone comes along

But the scar remains

And sometimes that scar
Continues to cause pain
Long after stitches are removed
Phantom pains of lost appendages
And lost wars

And sometimes
Often innocently
Or inadvertently
The one trying to fix
and care
and tend
to the scar
Is not the person who placed the scar there

And sometimes that scar
Causes phantom pains for *them*

And now
Somehow You
You, the patient, the healing, the scarred
are left in the position
Of apologizing
For a pain
You didn't inflict on yourself
But somehow have inflicted on them

You find yourself apologizing for a wound
You would rather not have had

And yet, here you are
Sometimes well scarred over
Sometimes still seeping with the blood

Standing in front of an innocent
Apologizing for a wound
Neither of you wish was there
(Really, aren't you an innocent, too?)

And which neither of you can take away

Despite how desperately you wish you could
At least not wholly
At least not right now

Holly Welker
Surrender

Futile, gazing at the sand-colored rocks
of some holy city and the loopy signature
of a friend who says she loves you from there.
You need to go look at something large,
the Grand Canyon perhaps. Stand right
next to the edge. Make someone hold onto you if
you're scared. You should be scared.

From the rim of the Grand Canyon there is much
you cannot see. Still you will find
mud and donkey shit all mixed up with
intolerable beauty and the conviction
that we live in a universe more stark, discrete
and varied than five weak senses can know.

Your own body, for instance. You know its odors,
its curves and hollows. But you'll never see
blood cells in your brain clustered in collages
so beautiful they terrify. And sometimes your heart
beats so loud you ask yourself, *When's this racket
gonna quit?* As if another noise, more
persistent still, might not take its place.

After all we are citizens of paradox, as morose
as statues of husky Christians and more perplexed
than a shaft of light making its twisted way
through the streets of Bologna. While
at a lake in China it's morning, everything bathed
in shadow. And always the stars, remote and
non-threatening, make you feel small
but not afraid. You need to feel afraid.

You need to be shocked by something large.
You need to see it and surrender. You need
to make your surrender an act of defiance.

In that peculiar nation of wonder, listen
as something tolls out the hours of the morning:
a distant fugue, scarce and compelling.
From that place love no one. Come home
and love us all.

Keira Shae
Newfound Religion

I saw Jesus once
outside my house
on a hot summer day of sales
drinking from my hose bib oh-so-quietly.
I was afraid
and I didn't offer him a cup
and closed my door.
I saw Jesus once
talking to himself
on the corner of the Parkway
and State Street
and I was afraid
and I didn't offer Him an ear.
I was too late for church.
Jesus stopped talking.
The Book stopped singing.
The clouds came
and I grew a desperate darkness
inside of me.
So I bought the hungry, pregnant Jesus
an All-you-can-eat buffet
on Sunday.
And I laughed under a tree with Toothless Jesus
as He sat on His only home with me.
I put a ring on my left hand
and climbed into bed with Jesus.
I told him I was sorry for my harsh words
after a very long Tuesday.
And in the middle of the night
Jesus cried out to me,
hungry and alone.
I got him all cleaned up
and I offered him some milk,
singing tenderly,
and I thanked Him for

coming to me again.
I promised I wouldn't ever
shut my eyes to Him again.

Coral Rose Goplin
(eve)

the holiest book introduced
the first female character
eve
defined by her position
creationrelation
to man
his rib
what even is that?
it's more like the punch line
of a joke
than a history

her role doesn't get better
without any women
to pass the bechdel with
she falls to chatting with the serpent
it's more gossip, really,
secrets hiding in forbidden
fruit.

i mean.
what really did He expect?
apparently women being told
that choices are death
as a deterrent
has been since
evening and morning
the first day
stealing
the ability to make life
choices
is nothing new

and so she does

and he follows her, adam
one of the few actions of hers
he won't take/be given
credit for

it's all her
this woman You gave me
*side eye from *this woman**
i mean.

Heather Harris-Bergevin

In my Father's house, there are many
mansions, but all
I need is one, small mansion
with green cabinets, and storage enough
for my canning jars, victoria strainer,
sewing machines and thread.

In my Father's house there are
many mansions, but all I want is
one cabinet with the right ratio of depth to being
able to find whatever is in the back of it.

In my Father's
house, there are many mansions,
but what is a mansion anyway? I need
electricity and running
water, air conditioning, and maybe
a peach tree in the yard.

In my Father's house there
are many mansions, but I need to sweep
mine, and maybe
put away some folded clothes.

In my Father's house there are many mansions, but
all I want is happy people talking
about funny memes, and chirpy
purring kittens being told
to get off the table because they
know better.

In my Father's house, there are many
mansions, but mine is
already established and sounding
with windchimes and laughter
and bookshelves.

And in my Father's house, where there are
many mansions, my heaven is
in tinycute houses, and the ability
to vacuum in one fell swoop, on one
floor, and decent attic space.

Laura Leigh
The Return
(2017)

When the Father God came,
his daughters lined up:
nails trimmed,
hairs ribboned.
shoulders straight,
bellies drawn.
Perfectly poised, yes.

Their dresses were starched
and precisely the right length.
neither too long
nor too short
Curves and contours concealed, check.

They smiled,
but not out loud.
Careful to mind The Balance.

When the Mother God arrived,
she found them reciting verses
in a perfectly straight row.

She said, Sweet Jesus, not again.
You don't have to do this, darlings—
go outside; play.
The trees are beckoning.

So they tore off their dresses,
tore through the orchards naked.
bellowing
hollering
galloping
laughing so wildly the clouds smiled.

They pissed in the bushes,
bludgeoned their knees,
tattooed themselves with bloodmud.
Declared themselves warriors
with armies of inchworms
To Battle! they cried—
and not quietly.

They conquered the stone walls,
then Juniper Peak,
then jumped from the cliffs to the river.
Gulped potions of wildwater,
and lay 'neath the sky
curls snarled
nails torn
nipples erect
alive.

The Father God looked from the window
and frowned.
They're wild as wolves, he said,
watching them clamber up sycamores
blood dripping down their chins.

The Mother God looked from the window
and laughed.
She walked toward the back door
kicked off her shoes
and said
Go fuck yourself, Marvin.

Mark Jeffreys
Throwing Shade

"The fabulist only wants
To dramatize, but the fraud
Wants to deceive." That's one way
We deceive ourselves,

One among many.
We'd like to believe we can
Discern moral distinctions

Between the storyteller
True of heart and the liar
Kicked to the curb, but they're blurred.

There's a shadow in all tales:
Truth savors its deceptions.
There's no shelter without shade,
No faith without corrections.

Holly Welker
Portrait of a Bedtime Storyteller

I would like to introduce myself by subtle and artful means.
I would like to insinuate myself into this conversation.
I'll be your hostess tonight.
It's years since I've been in either a quandary or a choir.
I'm a drain on society. I'm a flanneuse. I'm a bedtime storyteller,
and boy can I dance, having lived a long time as a contortionist,
which granted me dexterity and a certain suppleness of limb.

Once the blurry Atlantic hinged to the continent I stood on
reminded me of Viking ships: the spines curved up and ribbed
with tight, close planks, the jaws and teeth of the figureheads,
long necks endlessly intertwining along the hulls, a fleet
that hiked the rim of the world without offering an excuse,
nervy the way talented amateurs often are,
people with all ten fingers and restless fingers
at that, fingers that switch on the light
at five a.m. and make sure SOMEONE wakes up—

I know what you want to ask.
"What about that salacious hagiographer? The one who lived
among the damned though most of his relatives were saints?
What about that refractory renegade sorceress, the umpteenth
ingenue seduced by a tangle of rose bushes and a goldfish pond?"

But I didn't go out looking for this profession; I fell into it, victim
of an excellent memory and a horror of boredom. I can sit up
         straight
and pay attention on both a barstool and a church pew, but I'm
         lousy
at flirting and lousier at saying *amen*. If you want to be
amused or sanctified, I learned long ago, you've got to be willing
to do it yourself, and most people forget not only
their mother's birthday but what happened next.

This is where it gets complicated. Like everyone else, I inherited

lies that weren't meant to be lies, mistakes nobody fixed,
naughtiness and power, and I gave my heart to know wisdom,
to know madness and folly. I have humility to spare
but not enough arrogance, and I say that sincerely.
I want to rove in search of plunder, or at least a decent view.
I don't think having your heart broken is something you *need*
to fear, as opposed to wild dogs or dark foreign alleys
teeming with weirdos. It's like stage fright: you get up
and recite a monologue of Blanche Dubois' or play
your saxophone or whatever, even if you're scared shitless.
No matter how you prepare, you might still blow it.
There's never a Temple of Music and Art where it's a sure thing
no torrent of blue boredom and disbelief
will roll off the audience and quash you like a yawn.

A good retort can be used for distillation, sublimation,
or decomposition by heat. I've rebelled against those nights
when, yawning and brushing my teeth, I muttered to myself
about hooligans I got stuck with in the past.
As soon as I wake now I start planning the next night's dreams,
inchoate schedules of possibility. I tell stories so I can conjure
a few dozen guardian angels to flit about my basement
and keep cobwebs away. How long has the hollow of my thigh
been out of joint? I know my soul has a watermark, a translucent
        stamp
you can see only when you hold me up to the light.
Still, for a soothsayer I can be pretty darn dense.
For a sorceress I can be awfully plain. But there's nothing
I want to impose on another by coercion or trickery
and anyway, spells aren't straightforward: *cast* doesn't just mean
to throw; it also means *to contrive, devise, to warp, to twist*,
while *conspecific* means *of the same species* and when will I
ever use that? I'm undismayed by everything but insomnia
and what I hate most is being disinterred from sleep.
Someone else must save the elephants I can only
mourn. Someone else must watch football.
I leave those tasks alone. In the meantime, I can say
anything I want. Anything. As in "Any life is worth at least a
        stone"

94 SHADES OF BECOMING

or "We would all do well to love the word *shameless*."

Conspecific: things rub off when you stick them together, like pain
and snowmen. It's a countryside decorated with
heart-shaped gardens and the torsos of willowy women.
What I can tell you is that signs ought to give you an option,
a chance to ignore them if you like, a moment to push back
your hair and mutter, "maybe." If there's no choice about signs
then there's nothing special about *grace*, the irresistible force
that carves a notice on the heart announcing
in barely legible letters long, long after he's gone
and the details of his visit are even less distinct than
the reasons for it that *God was here*,
God, that curious restless tourist
who always thinks he needs to leave a mark.

I'm out of here. Fled. Here are my hands.
They decorate themselves with silver and amber and lapis,
they horde solitude as if it were chocolate or polished stones.
They fold themselves in attitudes of prayer, and they
are disconsolate, pious liars. *Listen*, I say,
and everyone in my dream listens, imagining a child asleep,
bare red trees and the moon rising over dirty snow:
and they wait for silence or for someone to say
It's going to be all right.

Mette Ivie Harrison
All Alone

When it strikes you for the first time as an adult
That the most likely truth is that we're alone.
All of us, alone in the universe.
That there isn't a God and there probably aren't
Aliens out there, either,
Waiting to talk to us because they're lonely, too,
And they think that we're smart enough to be interesting.

There's no going back.
Once you know the truth, there's only one thing left to do.
To get used to being alone.
To practice it. With meditation.
And long runs alone, on the treadmill or in the mountains.

The universe is such a big place to be alone in.
It's not just rattling around in an old house.
There's a vastness there, and an emptiness.
We who live on a planet forget how much of space is nothingness.
And we tell ourselves we're not really alone,
Because there are other animals, and species, and well,
Maybe there are still aliens.
So we maybe get a dog or a cat, and turn on some music to forget.

Jeremy C. Young
The Atheist's Creed

I don't believe in God.
But—
If God is the sum total of all souls in harmony with one another,
        if God is the experience of the numinous,
        if God is what we mean when we say love,
        well, I believe in that.
If God is the part of all of us that seeks oneness with nature
        and community with other people,
        if God is the part of us that weeps at suffering and injustice,
        if God is the *best* part of us,
        I believe in that, too.
So I guess, even though I don't believe in God,
        maybe I do.

If you think Jesus was divine,
        then count me out.
But—
What does it mean to be divine?
If it means bringing together people from all walks of life,
        anyone who would listen,
        and teaching them to love one another,
        well, Jesus did that.
If it means devoting one's life to proving there's a better way to
        live,
        urging people to put aside their selfishness
        and build a whole society based on love,
        Jesus did that, too.
So I guess, even though I don't believe Jesus was divine,
        maybe I do.

I'm not a member of any church.
But—
If joining a church means meeting in fellowship with others
        to share our spiritual journeys,
        if it means making music together,

celebrating the passing of the seasons together,
watching our children grow up together,
well, I do that.
If joining a church means caring for the poor and the friendless,
if it means not being satisfied with injustice,
if it means working to build the world Jesus envisioned everywhere
and right here at home,
I try to do that, too.
So I guess, even though I'm not a member of any church,
maybe I am.

I'm not a Christian.
Or am I?
Because it seems to me
that what I call love
you call God.
What I call loving thy neighbor
you call divinity.
What I call building the beloved community
you call church.
Are we saying the same thing, you and I,
in different languages?
Is the leaping feeling in my chest
the same as the one in yours?
And if so—
if so—
am I a Christian, too?

Mark Jeffreys
Grandma Cottonwood

If faith is arbitrary,
Let it be. I'll choose my own.
I'll make it ridiculous,

I'll make it feckless, shameless,
Pointless to proselytize,
Too damned absurd to believe,

And serve as my own martyr.
Why not? I'll worship a tree.
Not just any tree of course

But a grand, unusual,
Great tree, personal to me:
The cottonwood up the road.

I'll anthropomorphize her,
Treat her as both family
And all-knowing matriarch.

My prime article of faith
Is that She listens to me,
And responds to me in signs.

She watches me and helps me.
She created my whole world.
Her shade and my faith are one.

Kristen R. Shill
holy

i asked the goddess to
absolve me
sanctify
make me
holy

she brushed the
the sticksandstones
from my hair

darling
i already made you
wholly

Laura Leigh
The Mother's Prayer
(2016)

Our Goddess,
who art in the trees,
hallowed be thy name
which we like to think is Sylvia.
Thy queendom come,
Thy will be done,
(And we know thy will is for us to smash the patriarchy.)

Give us this day our daily fucks;
for we are all out.
All out, Goddess.
Our toddlers don't let us sleep,
and they whine all the way to daycare,
and they kick and scream and holler like banshees when we try to
drop them off,
because they give no shits if we're late to work.
Not a single shit, Goddess.

Lead us not into temptation,
because even though our bosses stare at our breasts
and ask us to fetch them coffee,
we know that stabbing them would be wrong
If only because it would hurt our ability to rise in power and
influence in our vocations,
And make the world safer patch of soil for marginalized persons.

Deliver us from judgment of sanctimonious parents
who only give their kids organic, garden-grown oatmeal,
and home-made, shaman-blessed goat's cream.
Because Cheerios aren't *that* bad; amiright, Goddess in The
Trees?
In the name of the aspen, and the magnolia, and the holy nachos,
Amen.

Kristen R. Shill
Eostre

She is risen.
new life a reflection of Her glory,
She, the peaceweaver
rebukes death and destruction
with Her healer's hands
touched the scorched earth and said "It is finished."
She whispered the words of life to Her Son's body,
She is despised and rejected of men.
She is risen,
the velvet bloom of the flowers Her handiwork.
She speaks peace to the raindrops,
life upon life, everlasting.
She feathers the wings of the thrush,
teaches the robin its songs.
She is the sunlight and the starlight,
the rust of the Blue Ridge Mountains
and the swell of the oceans.
She is risen.

Keira Shae
The Cathedral

My first silhouette
in my infancy
was the cathedral windows
with their pointed tops.
I stood tiptoed
in the poorly tended grass
for a peek of the faces
that made such lovely sounds.
Their mouths made the same shape
as the windows that caught
the fog of my breath,
and I felt they were holy.

I wandered far from
that brick and grass
but never forgot the shape.
I found myself near Great Waters.
Ships brought nourishment
and lovers home from
journeys abroad.
Along my way, a merry couple reunited.
Their hesitant hands found each other, as if needing tangible
          evidence of existence.
Their lovely pair
—one rough one smooth—
greeted each other
and made the same shape.
And I felt they were holy.

Many years later
I lived among strange
and difficult terrain,
high above the towns.
Two brothers, hot with anger,
attacked one another.

The smaller of the two,
in desperation,
secured a large stone.
Stunned, my breath caught
as I saw the same silhouette
made by the length of his arms...
as well as the peak behind him.
The shape dissipated,
and I felt it was holy.

Short on supplies,
I was hired help for a small farm
about to receive their first child.
I heard the wailing
as I rose at dawn.
I heard the groaning
as I plucked the chickens.
I heard nothing
as I brought the soup.
By candlelight I beheld a sacred scene;
forehead to forehead,
mother and child,
both had survived the day's undertaking.

I saw the cathedral yet again.
And it was holy.

Laura Leigh
The Plan of Salvation, Revised
(2015)

Sometimes, when you sleep, child,
I hold your head to my breast
and whisper love into your hair.
I hold your body and can't breathe
and I whisper salty tears into your hair.
I sing You are My Sunshine
but only the first verse, because the second makes you cry.

Bone of my bone and flesh of my flesh
Enzymes of my enzymes—that's not as poetic, I suppose,
but you love to hear about how bodies work.
What would we do without each other, child?
I don't like to think about it.
But I do, because I'm your mother, see.
And because you ask me every night
What if I die?
What if you die?

I used to have a lot of answers
but everything changed and,
darling,
I don't know anything anymore.

But here's a mother's promise,
the best I can do.
If I lose you, God forbid,
I'll plant a tree, and sprinkle some of your ashes in the soil.
The tree will grow with pieces of you—
Your chemicals and molecules and nucleic acids.
I'll plant daisies and daffodils,
and I'll sit by my Tree Daughter and sing
You are My Sunshine—
(only the first verse, of course).

And you'll always be my little bug
and I'll love you for always
even though it will hurt to breathe.

And if you lose me, God forbid,
I'll be with you everywhere.
I'll be the ocean climbing over your toes,
the warm rain on summer mornings.
I'll be the silt that holds you up when you hike,
and the clouds rolling across the desert sky.
I'll be in the water and air and sky and fire,
and on cool evenings,
I'll whisper love into your hair in soft breezes.

I'll watch over your shoulder as your write stories and draw
        unicorns—
I'll be a helicopter angel mother.
When you're sad, little bug,
I'll call to you from the treetops
and say,
My glorious child,
Cry and cry and cry.
Sob until you are limp.
I'll breathe strength into your limbs.
I'll whisper courage into your veins.
I'll sing you lullabies in the dark.

I'll watch you from the treetops -
you on your bike; you icing cookies; you scraping your knees.
You laughing with your friends,
you chasing your sister around the dining table.

I'll watch you and cry Tree Mother tears and say
Good heavens, child,
You are magnificent.

Kristen R. Shill
A Heathen's Prayer

I need a prayer for the thirst
that comes from drinking from
empty glasses,

a prayer for thinking I was the problem

People, I need a prayer for the questions I thought I had answers

Give us a prayer for this year
we've run out of the words
for this sort of thing

Ibrahim had faith
but
I cannot name a bigger faith
than believing that this is as bad as it gets
and hanging around on the blind hope
that it could be better

I need a prayer for
getting better
a sturdy, machine-washable mantle
of hope that however
frayed around the edges
keeps the human soul
warm

Please write me a prayer for the good days
catechism of kindness to
roll between one's toes
what is holier than dust
and time

Darlings, be a prayer to one another
to the staying alive
to the costs of staying

to your frailties
and mine
this is my prayer

that you feel incandescently
enough
that we all may heal
this broken glorious place

together

amen

contributors

Alisa Bolander is a designer who loves to sing, skate, and use well-placed words to make her way through life. She lives in Sandy, UT with her husband and son.

Allison Ulrich enjoys the outdoors in non-winter weather. The beautiful state and national parks in Utah have helped her fall in love with her home. She enjoys volunteering in her community and also church hops as much as possible. Her grandest wish for her children is for them to be aware of and kind to others and themselves.

Brittany Sweeney-Lawson is a lover of writing in all it's myriad forms. She has been a regular contributor to the Young Mormon Feminists blog, and currently writes and edits The Noggin, a quarterly e-zine for brain injury survivors and their families. Her Mormon faith transition has included its share of tears, travails, and even odd moments of hilarity. These poems are the culmination of her working through her complicated feelings of exiting Mormonism, and religion in general (for now). For what it's worth, she hopes they make anyone who reads them feel less alone and more understood as they undergo their own journeys of faith.

C.M.Blanco is a cis queer feminist cultural Mormon. She was born and raised a second generation member of The Church of Jesus Christ of Latter-day Saints in Spain, but has also lived and studied in England. She is a theatre researcher and practitioner whose main research areas include representations of religious belief on stage, cultural adaptation, and Early Modern Drama.

Cat Roebuck wrestled with God through poetry until God left the arena. Raised in seven countries with Mormonism standing in as her home town, Cat has spent the last decade unraveling her faith and finding, in the process, peace. Now a grateful atheist living in Idaho, Cat dances it out, cooks without recipes, builds websites, meditates, takes pictures, delights in lazy Sundays with her family, friends, and cats, and tries to meet her children's questions with curiosity and science.

Coral Rose Goplin: I am a woman with a life full to the brim. I carry with me some big griefs, which are balanced with the huge joys of small humans and the hard everyday work of making a better world for them. I have an advanced degree in three dead languages, and despite a career in tech, none of them are computer languages. Surprised by the deep well of power found by binding my life truths into poems, I am deeply honored to be a part of this collection.

Heather Harris-Bergevin's book, *Lawless Women*, was published in 2018 by BCC Press, which took a risk that people might, indeed, bother to read modern feminist retellings of fairytales, even ones that don't even rhyme. Apparently, people _do_ like them, and she's terribly grateful. Heather lives in SC with three kids, two cats, a pile of rose bushes, and about fifteen bazillion mosquitoes. She edits for money, and sews and crafts for fun, except sometimes when she does that the other way around. She likes her forties WAY better than her thirties.

Holly Welker is a fourth-generation native Arizonan. She grew up in a small town so Mormon that the high school prom was always held in the cultural hall of the local LDS meetinghouse. Her ancestors arrived in Utah with Brigham Young. She is the editor of *Baring Witness: 36 Mormon Women Talk Candidly about Love, Sex, and Marriage*. Her poetry, fiction, essays, journalism and scholarship have appeared in dozens of publications, including *Best American Essays*, *Bitch*, *Dialogue: A Journal of Mormon Thought*, *The Iowa Review*, *Poetry International*, *Slate*, and *The New York Times*.

J. Marie Murphy is a writer and adventurer. She brings her experiences from growing up around the world, the unexpected lessons she learned as a classroom teacher, and her time in the corporate world into her writing. Her work is often tied to her religious upbringing and deep-seated spirituality. When not writing or adventuring, you can find Marie walking her dog, cheering on her local soccer team (Real Salt Lake), or trying a new recipe.

Jeannine Robinett was a lifelong Mormon who realized that to save her spirituality she had to take a break from the church. She found a Unitarian Universalist church where her soul could blossom and where she was challenged to retain and reclaim the best parts of her Mormon heritage. She begins seminary at Meadville Lombard Theological School in the fall of 2019.

Jennith Lucas is a disabled and queer ex-Mormon mother, student, and worker. She currently lives in Syracuse, New York with her two children, their cat Maude, and ample grad school angst. Whenever she drinks at parties, she likes to loudly process her exit from Mormonism.

Jeremy C. Young is an assistant professor of history at Dixie State University. An enrolled Unitarian Universalist, he has worked as a musician at Catholic and Episcopal churches and has attended United Church of Christ and Community of Christ congregations. He lives in St. George, Utah, with his wife, Chelsea McCracken, an assistant professor of interdisciplinary studies at DSU.

Josie Chilton lives in Spanish Fork Utah with her family. She spends most of her time avoiding items on her to-do-list in favor of more creative pursuits. Recently these pursuits have become outlets for the difficult emotions of a faith transition. She's also a pretty impressive backwards talker.

Despite having a profoundly abusive childhood at the hands of a Meth-addict mother, **Keira Shae** is a joyful, healthy, college-educated, thriving woman. She credits her Mormon neighbors as a large part of the reason she's still alive today. In addition to her published memoir, *How The Light Gets In*, she is also happily married to Nicholas Scholz, and together they have three sons.

Kristen R. Shill is a professional word gatherer, yarn wrangler, and bath witch. After majoring in Reading Stuff and taking a detour to law school, she decanted a loinfruit who didn't sleep for three years. Like her heroes Ron Swanson and Leslie Knope, she believes in the healing powers of breakfast.

.

Maren N. Chen grew up in eastern Oregon and moved to Utah at the age of 21. She earned a Bachelor of Arts in Art History and French from the University of Oregon, and a Master of Arts in Languages and Literature from the University of Utah. Maren has worked as an Instructor of French and of English as a Second Language. She currently lives in Salt Lake City Utah, with her husband and their two children and one cat. In addition to writing poetry and essays, Maren is obsessed with refurbishing picture frames, reading French philosophy, and all things Anne of Green Gables.

Mark Jeffreys grew up in a large, evangelical Baptist family in New Jersey in the 1960s and 70s. In his teens he attended the Stony Brook School, a Christian boarding academy. In his twenties he taught at Morehouse College, the alma mater of Dr. Martin Luther King, Jr. He holds doctorates in English and Evolutionary Anthropology, and he currently teaches at Dixie State University.

Mette Ivie Harrison writes the Linda Wallheim mystery series set in Draper, Utah (*The Bishop's Wife*), as well as young adult fantasy (*The Princess and the Hound*). She wrote regularly for Huffington about Mormonism and faith from 2015-2017 and writes occasionally for RNS. She holds a PhD in Germanic Languages and Literatures from Princeton and is an All-American triathlete and mother of five. She is new to poetry.

Nancy Ross is an assistant professor in the Interdisciplinary Arts and Sciences Department at Dixie State University, where she has been teaching for 12 years. Her degrees are in art history but she moonlights as a sociologist of religion. She recently co-edited a book with Sara K.S. Hanks titled *Where We Must Stand: Ten Years of Feminist Mormon Housewives* (2018). She is also an ordained elder and pastor for Community of Christ.

Sarah Broat is a UX Designer living in Omaha, Nebraska with her fiancée Amanda, dog, and three cats. She became a Latter-day Saint in her early 20s and checked off all of the boxes—Church school, endowment, and a temple marriage—before life circumstances took her down a different path. Sarah is still active and believing, but now has a more nuanced faith.

Stephanie Sorensen is a lover of many things, including writing, reading, sleeping in, Navajo tacos, and being outdoors. Her four children and small business pursuits (bodhibirthservices.com) keep her on the move, but when she can slow down she loves to travel, spend time with her husband, and just sip a steamy hot beverage on her back patio. She's learning to love the ebbs and flows, highs and lows, of her life and looks forward to a whole new variety of adventures that await her. Life is so, so good.

Susan Meredith Hinckley is an AZ artist/writer, and a graduate of the University of Utah. She enjoys desert living, creating the webcomic *Gray Area*, long walks, short runs, and endless examination of both her faith and her lack thereof.

Laura Leigh grew up in the hills of Northern Utah where her love of alpine lakes, quaking aspen, and mountain bluebells has decidedly not translated into an ability to grow a garden. She is an environmental engineer-turned-molecular immunologist who has researched watershed conservation, immune responses to pathogens, and epigenetic regulation of neuroinflammation. Laura currently lives in Salt Lake City with her husband, two daughters, and dozens of dying succulents.